IN THE SAND

The TOTALLY AWESOME guide to ANIMALS

By Brenda McHale

BookLife PUBLISHING

©2023
BookLife Publishing Ltd.
King's Lynn
Norfolk, PE30 4LS, UK

All rights reserved.
Printed in Poland.

A catalogue record for this book is available from the British Library.

ISBN: 978-1-80155-650-7

Written by:
Brenda McHale

Edited by:
Emilie Dufresne

Designed by:
Dan Scase

All facts, statistics, web addresses and URLs in this book were verified as valid and accurate at time of writing. No responsibility for any changes to external websites or references can be accepted by either the author or publisher.

PHOTO CREDITS

All images are courtesy of Shutterstock.com. With thanks to Getty Images, Thinkstock Photo and iStockphoto. Front page – Alexandra Lande. 4&5 – hagit berkovich, Viktor Loki, Pavel Krasensky, Matt Knoth. 6&7 – Carlos Amarillo, Roger de la Harpe, shflickinger. 8&9 – Roman Gilmanov, Arnoud Quanjer, OMMB, Protasov AN. 10&11 – Chantelle Bosch, Willem van de Kerkhof. 12&13 – Roger de Montfort, Earth Stories Photography. 14&15 – Shengyong Li, Vera Larina, meunierd, Anan Kaewkhammul, Inc. 16&17 – Photo by Greg Hume CC-BY-2.5, Derrick Coetzee. 18&19 – Sergei25, NATURE WEB, volkova natalia. 20&21 – Owen65, Chris Watson, Pacific Southwest Region USFWS. 22&23 – Milan Zygmunt, Ken Griffiths, Artush, Danita Delmont, Andre Coetzer.

CONTENTS

PAGE 4	What Lives in the Sand?
PAGE 6	Meerkat
PAGE 8	Scorpion
PAGE 10	Shovel-Snouted Lizard
PAGE 12	Namaqua Chameleon
PAGE 14	Camel
PAGE 16	Honeypot Ant
PAGE 18	Dorcas Gazelle
PAGE 20	Desert Spadefoot Toad
PAGE 22	Wacky Wildlife
PAGE 24	Glossary and Index

Words that look like this can be found in the glossary on page 24.

WHAT LIVES IN THE SAND?

It can be hard to live in the heat of the desert. But here are some types of creature that can survive there:

Mammals such as fennec foxes

Reptiles such as short-horned lizards

Insects such as Sahara desert ants

On each page you will see a fact file like this. It will tell you lots of things about the animal, such as what type of animal it is, its <u>diet</u> and where it lives.

COYOTE

Type: Mammal
Found: North and Central America
Diet: Other small mammals

MEERKAT

Some meerkats look out for danger. They can use six different barks or whistles to tell other meerkats if there is danger.

MEERKAT
Type: Mammal
Found: Africa
Diet: Insects, lizards and fruit

One type of whistle will tell everyone to run down the burrow. A different whistle tells them how far away the danger is.

Meerkats sleep in a big pile to keep warm.

Meerkats can close their ears to keep the sand out.

Meerkats have an extra eyelid that covers their eyes when they dig.

When a meerkat parent needs to leave their home, a babysitter will look after the baby meerkats.

SCORPION

Some scorpions can survive up to a year without eating or drinking.

In some lights, scorpions can glow in the dark.

SCORPION

Type: Arachnid
Found: Deserts, forests and mountains
Diet: Insects, small reptiles and animals

NAME/NOM: In the Sand

A baby scorpion rides on its mother's back when it's first born. But if a scorpion mother gets hungry, she might choose to eat her babies.

Scorpions that have smaller pincers are usually more venomous.

Small pincers

SHOVEL-SNOUTED LIZARD

The shovel-snouted lizard runs at nearly one metre per second.

SHOVEL-SNOUTED LIZARD

Type: Reptile
Found: Namib desert
Diet: Small insects

It dances on hot sand. It lifts two legs up then the opposite two. This stops its feet from overheating.

Shovel-snouted lizards have two <u>bladders</u>. One is for wee. The other is used to store water.

Other animals like to catch this lizard because it's like a water bottle for them.

NAMAQUA CHAMELEON

NAMAQUA CHAMELEON
Type: Reptile
Found: Africa
Diet: Small insects and other reptiles

In the morning, Namaqua chameleons turn dark grey. This helps them to <u>absorb</u> heat from the Sun to warm up.

As it gets hotter throughout the day, the chameleon turns white to help it stay cool.

Dark colour in the morning

Light colour in the heat of the day

12

Namaqua chameleons dig holes to reach cool sand and escape the desert heat.

Its tongue is longer than its whole body, and is sticky on the end.

CAMEL

Camels say hello by blowing in each other's faces.

CAMEL
Type: Mammal
Found: Africa and Asia
Diet: Different types of plants

Camels are known for spitting up the contents of their stomachs at something that might be threatening them.

You can tell when a camel is about to spit because they huff and their cheeks bulge.

A camel can drink over 100 litres of water in 15 minutes. That's the same as half a bath full of water.

Camels moan, groan and bellow. Some of these noises were used to create Chewbacca's voice from the Star Wars films.

Camels can sit on really hot ground because they have thick skin on their knees and chest.

HONEYPOT ANT

HONEYPOT ANT

Type: Insect
Found: North and Central America, Africa and Australia
Diet: Nectar and other insects

Some honeypot ants hang from the nest ceiling while other ants feed them nectar until they look like juicy grapes.

When the other ants need food, they stroke the grape-sized ants' antennae and they sick the food back up.

Honeypot ants have been known to attack other honeypot ant colonies. They try and steal the grape-sized ants full of sugary juice.

Some people like to eat the ants as a sweet treat.

DORCAS GAZELLE

DORCAS GAZELLE

Type: Mammal
Found: Africa
Diet: Plants and small insects

The dorcas gazelle doesn't have to wee. In very dry weather, its wee can come out as a dry lump of white stuff.

The dorcas gazelle can get all the water it needs from what it eats.

When being chased by an attacker, dorcas gazelles jump high in the air to warn other gazelles and show the attacker how fit they are.

Male dorcas gazelles make piles of poo to mark their area.

DESERT SPADEFOOT TOAD

DESERT SPADEFOOT TOAD

NAME/NOM: *In the Sand*

Type: *Amphibian*
Found: *Australia*
Diet: *Small creatures*

The tadpoles of desert spadefoot toads sometimes eat other tadpoles in their group.

The toad's back feet are shaped like digging spades. They even have a sharp edge on them.

Spadefoot toad tadpoles grow very quickly so they are ready to leave the pool they are in before it dries up in the hot desert weather.

Desert spadefoot toad tadpole

These toads dig down into the sand so that they don't get too dry. They are usually only seen above ground after it has rained.

21

WACKY WILDLIFE

Young tiger salamanders eat each other. But they can tell which ones are their brothers and sisters and so don't eat them.

Sidewinder snakes move sideways on the sand. This is so their bodies do not touch the hot sand for too long.

Cape ground squirrels use their bushy tails to give them shade from the hot sun.

Geckos lick their own eyeballs to clean sand off.

The horned lizard squirts blood out of its eyes to defend itself from attackers.

GLOSSARY

absorb	to take in or soak up
amphibian	an animal that can live both on land and in water
antennae	a pair of long, thin sensors found on the heads of insects
arachnid	a type of animal that has eight legs, such as spiders and scorpions
bladders	things in animals and humans that hold wee
diet	the kinds of food that a person or animal usually eats
insects	animals with six legs, no backbone and usually one or two pairs of wings
mammals	animals that are warm blooded, have a backbone and produce milk to feed their children
nectar	a sweet liquid made by plants
nest	something made by an animal to live in and keep it safe and warm
reptiles	cold-blooded animals with scales
venomous	able to poison another animal through a bite or a scratch

INDEX

babies 7, 9, 20–22
blood 23
burrows 6
digging 7, 13, 20–21

ears 7
eyes 7, 23
legs 10
nectar 16

sand 4, 7, 10, 13, 21–23
tongues 13
water 11, 15, 18